Let Go of the Hands You Hold

Marissa Glover's *Let Go of the Hands You Hold* is the work of a poet with perfect pitch, a powerful testament to the violence we have endured and our rebellion against cruelty. Themes of loss, love, motherhood, grief, identity, and memories interweave throughout with high-spirited clarity. Erudite, heart-wrenching, and multifaceted, this masterfully crafted collection delivers a daringly personal rendering of contemporary reality and bears witness to the human capacity to persevere in a broken world.

—Hélène Cardona, author *Life in Suspension*

There is certainly whimsy in Marissa Glover's poems, but it is a whimsy with something at stake. These are poems on the edge, exploring the passions and frustrations of the body with humor and pathos. At their best, they are angry without being bitter, funny without being flippant, tender without being sentimental. "Discover what you love most about creation," she writes. "It is good. It is good." And these poems make their way to that praise.

—Joseph Fasano, author of *The Dark Heart of Every Wild Thing*, *The Crossing*, and *Vincent*

Marissa Glover's *Let Go of the Hands You Hold* is a full-tilt run at what it means to inhabit a female body—to own it, wear it, wield it, to suffer its pains and inherit its urges and cautions in a world that feels more tightrope than freeway. Glover asks us to question cultural norms and bear witness, whether it's interrogating our roles in society or eschewing the legacy of misogyny as she points a velvet glove in its direction. Whatever Glover's experience, there is a sense of resilience and pragmatism throughout. Even when she considers the practical uses of poetry, we are reminded of its power to "wrap words / around my body like a cast, setting what's broken / so it can heal." Where "poems are / like women—unseen, the work often unpraised, / done in dark hours without witness, necessary / as sleep, as blood, as air."

—Lois P. Jones, author of *Night Ladder*

LET GO OF THE HANDS YOU HOLD

Poems

Marissa Glover

MERCER UNIVERSITY PRESS
Macon, Georgia
2021

MUP/ P621

Published by Mercer University Press
1501 Mercer University Drive
Macon, Georgia 31207

25 24 23 22 21 5 4 3 2 1

Books published by Mercer University Press are printed on acid-free paper that meets the requirements of the American National Standard for Information Sciences—Permanence of Paper for Printed Library Materials.

Printed and bound in the United States.

This book is set in Adobe Caslon Pro.

Cover/jacket design by Burt&Burt.

Author photo by Benjamin Watters; photo editing by Stephanie Reed Photography

Library of Congress Cataloging-in-Publication Data

Glover, Marissa, 1974- author.
Let go of the hands you hold : poems / Marissa Glover.
Macon, Georgia : Mercer University Press, 2021. | Includes bibliographical references. |
LCCN 2020050716 | ISBN 9780881467826 (paperback)
LCGFT: Poetry.
LCC PS3607.L686 L48 2021 | DDC 811/.6--dc23
LC record available at https://lccn.loc.gov/2020050716

For my dad

MERCER UNIVERSITY

MERCER UNIVERSITY PRESS

Endowed by

TOM WATSON BROWN

and

THE WATSON-BROWN FOUNDATION, INC.

Contents

NB: For the poems marked with an asterisk, simply aim your smart phone camera at the QR Code printed on the page to hear Marissa deliver her spoken word piece.

Now, what
it's come down to finally
is this: light and shadow,
dark tree limbs, pale sky
a garden, and the need to tell
you, over and over, how it was.

—Adrienne Bond, "Script"

I.

The Happy Hour of Assault

No one writes poems about the guy
who changes your brake light when it burns

out, or snakes your soap-matted hair
from the drain. There's nothing romantic

about being nice. Nor do we write poems
for the husband who is now married

to someone who is not us. Poems
are for the men who send purple calla lilies

inscribed with lines from Neruda
and then treat you like shit.

We pick the prick just sharp enough
to spur our muse yet not so barbed

it draws blood.

Chair Envy

For insurance purposes, this
diagnosis should not be confused
with Penis Envy. See the DSM-5
for proper coding.

I envy the chair that holds you.
It doesn't even know
your name—yet
you indulge its purpose
casually, or sitting straight,
as if it knew you well
enough to touch you there.

Bigger Isn't Better

People always say size matters.

But these days it's hard
to know what's true, so I
studied the subject for myself—
to see if reports I'd heard
were just fake news.

Science says Frenchmen have
the largest members. And
M. Martin indeed insisted
his was best, and that I *kiss it!*
kiss it! kiss it! A frog with frantic
aim, he lashed about—a series
of this and that—quickly in,
quicker out. As if he meant to
whip a fly from the cervix wall,
he jerked his darting *bite*
faster than a blink. Note to self:
Get to know a man before you drink.

Lorenzo the Italian who experts said
should've measured second was hung
like Michelangelo's *David* but knew
exactly what to do. While Keith the poet
was Brobdingnagian and left me
sorely bruised. He'd proudly chant:
half a league, half a league, half a league
onward and expect me to salute.

No, the best lay of all my days
complained of Peyronie's disease
and bloomed in season like a Weeping
Willow, which just goes to show—
it's not the size of the bedpost that matters
but the fluff of the pillow.

Better than Sex

When my grandma tells me
there is a cake better than sex,
I don't believe her.

So she describes it—
I listen, still not believing,
watching her eyes water
at her words, her hands animate
the actions as she lists ingredients.

Better than sex,
she says, licking her lips,
which have dried in the telling.

Looking to the kitchen clock,
she clears her throat with a cough,
and gives me final instructions in staccato
as if reading from the yellowed recipe card
kept in her mother's tin on the stove:

Prep time: 30 minutes
Cook time: 1 hour
Ready: 1 hour 30 minutes

I ask, *Who has that kind of time?*

She sighs, *Exactly.*

His Skin a Gleaming Rust

Issued a travel visa to this
distant port, we enter this man's
fraternity of freckles, knowing
it's dangerous to trespass here,
where flesh conspires, knowing
others lost their way long before
they were dashed against the rocks.

Mapping currents with fingers,
tongue, tracing then tasting reds
and browns burnt into too-white skin,
a labyrinth of damaged cells, pigment,
hues—we choose the concave of elbow,
ride the swell of bicep flecked by sun,
settle on cobble lit in constellation,
a dangerous navigation.

His skin a gleaming rust of siren specks
that shift and dance on salted waves,
we're dizzied in mandalas. Baptized
without ceremony, we cry out
to silent gods and slip beneath the sea.

This Is My Body, Broken

In this sanctuary,
Woman regains her glory.
She is Eve
before the Fall, goddess of all
that is good and right, healer
of old wounds, weaver
of magic. She casts spells
to call forth seed.

The woman takes whatever
she's given and makes it pretty,
she makes all things pretty,
she is the Maker of Pretty.

She takes the man's dust
and salt and turns them into song.
She sets his skin in gold,
studs his bones with diamonds
until he shines. Her power dazzles,
quiets the devils shrieking
in his ear. This is grace

made flesh. Watch the woman offer
the fruit of her vine; watch the man
drink himself toward drowning.
The woman whispers,

This is my body, broken for you.
The man takes and eats
and will not remember.

The Problem with Us

You slink your way to me like a cat
proud of its catch, dead mouse dangling
from its bloodied jaws. You drop the poem
on my desk (so pleased you could purr)
folding sharp paws across your chest,
waiting for me to read what you've written
and reward you with a good petting.

The geography before me
recalls eras & armadas, a new
Age of Discovery. Flowers, oceans,
mountains—more with every vista.
The explorer's greed surges, fueling
the next wave of settlement, the need
to see what lies over each horizon—
everywhere to plant kisses like flags
of conquistadores, to say,
This, too, is mine.

History knows the conquistador
is defeated in the end. Explorers
are expedient. Their land will be
taken, flags trampled by boots
carrying other colors. Don't believe
the movies, the happy ending
with love that lasts.

In this story, as in every story, kisses
are replaced by blood. Everyone loses,
everything dies.

Externals

Because Julian Rotter was right
about the locus of control,
you keep running

the long course
toward *kotinos*, avoiding
the rocks you've strewn
across the path, while everyone
around you stumbles.

It's your dad's fault you didn't
take out the trash

your boss's fault you didn't
pay the insurance and

my fault my fault my fault

you boast the spineless
butcher's broom, odorous
reminders of the dizzying game
you play—this twisting words
into wreaths of perfectly placed

blame I was never meant to wear.

Appetites

I do not want the plum
until I see her eating it.

Close enough to hear
muted breaking of skin

as teeth puncture tender flesh,
my mouth aches

for the sweet tang
her mouth now tastes—

Even though after one bite,
I'd ache to spit it out.

Master of My Domain

I do what I want. I'm an American—
no asking if he's happy, not caring
if she's satisfied. I make my own way
in the world: Kick off the bed covers
or hide under sheets; stay silent or
scream. Maybe all of this. Maybe none.

In America, we're taught finishing first
is all that matters. Here, selfishness is
not a crime. You can't depend on anyone
else to make you feel good—a fact
you learned early, when your parents
split, when Mark Bowman's ambition
got him caught in a kickball double-play
to end the inning.

So you learn to please yourself,
now both explorer and native
land. Discover what you love most
about creation. It is good. It is good. It is—

Say your own name instead of God's
as you finish.

Robert Frost Said Poetry Is a Way of Taking Life by the Throat

So this is the phone call, the email
in the dark hours after everyone's gone
to bed, glass of wine on the nightstand
half full, words important as air.
This is the song Followill sings—
the melancholy one, the one that ends
with a smile, the one your wife plays
in the shower because she doesn't know
what it means. This is the apology—
an *I'm sorry* to appease the angels,
bypass the flaming swords barring us
from Eden, put the fruit back on the tree.

This is the sold sign planted in mud,
telling Shropshire the flat's been taken.
This is the job ad for a man who teases
fact from fog the way chefs on *Chopped*
cook complete meals from whatever
mystery ingredients are in the basket,
the way Fred Astaire dances
on the ceiling. This is the history book
teachers warn their class to read
with suspicion, eyes in search of bias
that leads to lies, penned by a poet
compelled to change the past, certain
a few good lines could write the future,
certain a future waits to be written,
certain the only story that ends happily
is the one that never ends.

Love Is Not Love

II.

I Dream I'm Cassandra

You should know better than to let a man inside you.
This story has been told to us for centuries.
Even as I repeat the warning, you do not listen.

A girl can lose herself in wise designs.
You grow dizzy. He knows; I know—everybody knows
but you. Because you still believe your city stands.

The man does not matter. Maybe tonight it is Epeius,
the carpenter, the boxer, good with hands—and fists.
Saturday night, Sinon the theologian says his offering

is for God as he enters your gates. All bear the same gift.
Pretending to surrender, doubling back as you sleep—
Tell me, what were you going to do with a hollow wooden horse?

A Taste for Naming

It started with Eve in the Garden.
A look, a taste of such delicious fruit—

Before the curse, names like *hamor*
and *gamel* rolled off Adam's tongue.

After, the taste for naming remained:
melons—grapefruits, lemons—
pear hips, orange peel thighs,
peach, pomegranate, cherry.

With this, man becomes master
of the garden. Paradise regained.

A lick of his lips, a whistle, a hiss.

How to Be a Pirate

after Gasparilla

Pin the prettiest girl at Plant. Take her dancing at the debutante's ball. Go to Duke. Pledge KA. Be a devil. Marry the president of Phi Mu. Make pretty babies. Be a doctor. Join Palma Ceia. Pay your dues. Buy a house on Blanca or Bayshore. Hire a pretty babysitter. Take the house in the divorce. Marry the babysitter. Play golf on Saturdays. Tennis on Tuesdays. Join the lodge before running for mayor. Make enough money to rub it in. Keep your gun and wingtips clean. Stock the crow's nest with bourbon and cigars before sailing. Paint your face with soot, wear a costume, pose for photographs. Invade the city that's already yours. Take whatever you want. Teach your sons and grandsons how much blood it takes to succeed, to make it all look real.

Every Man We've Ever Hated

The things we've vomited
will not be in the canon.

Call it art, call it protest—
this persistence, this
hashtag insistence,
is just us women, scratching
a name for ourselves
on history's bathroom stall
to say, *We were here.*
Somewhere Philomela
lost her tongue & she's tired
of being quiet.

Together
we write, we paint
with the only colors left—
Rosie Red & Pussy Pink.
We plug our bruises
into amplifiers. We grab
the microphone & we
motherfucking sing.

This is not resistance.
We have not enlisted.
We aren't jackdaws
or mockingjays. We are
nightingales & there
are bones inside
banging to get out.

Ink spills from every well,
floods the stage. At last,
we've been given
a single mark. We take
aim—emptying ourselves
of everything.

It's easier to hold one man
responsible for these wounds
than to catalog each crime
we've witnessed, recall faces
bleached from memory,
recount all the sins
still too sharp to name.

Holding It In

I fart and my son says I am gross.

He's been alive a decade, already
he's passing law: *Girls are not
allowed to fart.* Naturally, I protest:
You do it. Daddy does it too.
My logic is impeccable. He rebuts:
*This isn't sexism, Mom. It's just
a fact of life.*

And this is how it starts—
with farts. Teaching girls
to will it away
(never mind the damage)
or let it out in private
or express themselves quietly,
ladylike, so no one hears.

With the effort of Hercules,
we hold it all in—
stretching the intestines
pressuring the uterus
marching the stomach
into the throat, hiding everything
inside until we shut down

or explode.

The Worst Thing to Have Is a Vagina

You would snuff us out in the name of something holy,
controlling women's bodies like they belong to you
like you own them like you paid for them like I am my beloved's
but he is not mine—he is Solomon, King of the kingdom

and I am not wise enough to choose
so a male judge rules that doctors can keep cutting
women's bodies, even young girls who were tricked
into visiting the clinic—young girls too young to vote,

young girls too young to know men
will lie with their eyes wide open, with their hand over their heart
and on the Bible, will lie about anything—to win elections,
to make a deal, to get you to let down your guard

or your pants or this sacred dress you wear to honor the god
who men say made you wrong, made you to burn white-hot
and that is wrong, made you to swim with pleasure and that is
    wrong—
don't worry they will fix it, they will fix you

but they won't fix pregnant even if a man made you lie there
and take him, made you say thank you—pregnant is not a problem
you are the problem your vagina is the problem you need to say
    you're sorry
apologize for this body, apologize for wanting, apologize.

Woman in the Dock

She confesses her body
in blason prayer
heart, hands, mouth
a hymn to the Creator
lungs, soleus, wrist
reminding God
ears, ribs, breasts
that he once saw her naked
and decreed
It is good.

Politicking

Wait for the season
to plant—warm soil; water well.
The vine will take root.

Harvest carefully:
Yellow-brown, half-dead tendrils
means ripe for picking.

Hear a hollow thump?
Has the white belly yellowed?
With a sharp knife, cut.

Spoon out the black seeds—
fill the newspaper with them;
consider the pith.

Feast until you reach
the bitter rind; spit it out.
Use what's left for mulch.

Greetings from Helmand

When everyone else speaks of the weather
it's because they've nothing to say,
but when you report the rain
or describe how the moon waxes in the Afghan sky,
I know you mean something else
because *The Waste Land* is your favorite poem,
and only Pound and the Fisher King know what it's about.

The weather is not the weather.
Nothing is what it is unless it's also something more.
Life is difficult; each month the cruelest.
To survive, a man's got to know the meaning of things
and how to use his standard-issue SA80 A2.
You understand allusion and metaphor
and how to kill a man at a hundred metres.

When everyone else sends postcards from the desert—
lush field of poppies backed by distant snow-capped mountains
and *Dulce et decorum est pro patria mori*
scripted across the scene—to tell Mum and Dad
they've sent another raghead to hell, you email
on a secure line and ask if anyone will reach Elysium
now that you define "enemy" with both dictionary and mirror.

The Taliban have a word for enemy too.

History Is Now and England

Knuckles white—
tight on a turning wheel, plowing
across a bridge that spans four thousand years.

An overturned cart as collateral damage,
cut flowers litter the street like corpses—
carnations, tulips, poppies, hyssop.
Yarrow powder cannot stanch the bleeding.

Quiet hands clutch a brittle clay, searching
for sculptures lost to repeating winters—
the potter knows his work is wrecked.
Ishmael has come home to Isaac.
Sins of the father visit the sons.

We need the absent wind to blow.

If the President Asks About My Heritage

Tell him a six-month
membership at Ancestry
dot com connects me
to Vice President Dallas
and Signer John Hart
of New Jersey—tell him
these men make me
a Daughter of the Revolution.
Tell him what daughters do.
Tell him about the revolution.
Tell him DNA tests tie me
to Eleanor of Aquitaine.

But what is 1/1000
of anything? I'm dishes
piled in the sink, a ring
of pink at the toilet's
water line, a lone sock
in need of a match.
I'm pens without ink
forks without knives,
a single speck of dust
stuck in the eye.

Saliva tests all come back
the same—water and blood,
breath and bone—an old garden
overgrown with blame
part song, part sky, part snake.

Jesus Said

III.

Truth We Cannot Tell

Before they burn down our house
our bodies singed, the beds black dust

before they drag us 3.8 miles
behind a pickup truck down gravel road

before they tie us to a barbed wire fence,
beat us with baseball bats and a cattle prod

before they anoint us with honey
and plant us in the ground for ants

before they hang us from the southern
magnolia—wind chimes, a warning to others

they will break into our throat and rip out
the words too close to the tongue.

Life in the Time of Terror

after Manchester

I. Primary
The initial blast wave hits the body.
Barotrauma. Air-filled cavities are most susceptible:
Don't breathe. Cover your ears. Crouch down.

Only distance decides who lives and dies.
Pray for infinite kilometres.

II. Secondary
Airborne shrapnel penetrates the body.
Hardware is weaponized. If there were time,
you would recognize these metals.

Nails from the backyard tree house. Nuts and bolts
used to hang the television on the wall.

III. Tertiary
The body takes flight. Flesh and bone
recreated into missiles; children grow
into sledgehammers. No one is safe.

Let go of the hands you hold. Run.

IV. Quaternary
All that is not mind or spirit self-destructs.
Concrete collapses, crushing
those who cannot escape. Skin catches fire.
Smoke invades the lungs. Debris falls from the sky.

...

Beneath the survivor's guilt, doctors identify
cochlear damage and try to predict your future:
perilymph fistula? basilar membrane rupture?

But you won't know the extent of the damage
until "Bang Bang" plays on the radio fifteen years from now,
on a day your daughter might've married.

The World Asks Too Much of Mothers

I can't point to the place that hurts most.

No bruise or swelling,
no angry rash or cast—
it's closer to a cervix
opened beyond its bounds,
crowning, a jagged tear
through muscle. Blood
pools in secret places; unspooling
nerves tangle in a crooked seam
as pain is stitched
into every fitful sitting.

If God had asked Sarah
to make an offering of Isaac,
she would have laughed.
No march up the mountain.
No need for a ram in the thicket.
No obedience unto death.
God knew he better ask Abraham.

And we know better
than to be another Mary,
giving our son to die
for someone else's sin.
Because this world makes mothers
watch their children hang on trees
that do not lead to salvation.
We anoint our children for burials
that will not end in resurrection.

Unintended Consequences

With all the sadness in the news, I can't afford to mourn
each reported death. Such grief is unsustainable,
says my therapist. It's like Red Rover: Only the choosy side
survives. Send over the small stories, too weak to breach the wall
—don't call for suicides, bullets, bombs, children ripped
from their mother's arms. So I tap my collarbone like she taught
and chant, *I will not cry for people I do not know. I will not cry*
for people I do not know. I will not cry for people I do not know.
I will not cry—If you say it often enough, and with enough conviction,
you stop caring about people you don't know and even those you do.

Learning Beneficence

A golden spice pear tree
stands in my neighbor's yard
close to the property line.
When August wind blows
hard in my direction, a few
pears fall, hiding like Easter
eggs in overgrown grass—

The law would say
the fruit is now legally mine,
a kind of fortunate spoils.
Still, I gather the prodigals
before they rot, bag them,
drop them at my neighbor's door.

But there is more to charity
than giving, despite the optics
or what a preacher might say.
My therapist doesn't ask
why I return the pears; heaps
no praise on the woman
whose temptation's
rooted elsewhere.

Everyone Says They Saw the Signs

Some boys absorb their father's punches—
release them in sports or turn them into song.

Some store the hits in a bruised body, saving them
like pennies in a piggy bank, waiting to cash in
when the market's strong.

After the police leave, Ms. Smith talks to reporters
huddled at her mailbox, shoulder blades straining
to touch—a trick her mother taught her
for cotillion thirty years earlier,
long before the boy next door shot up the school.

Tonight, we'll hear the soundbite:
how it was just a matter of time, how he
pelted frogs as a kid, tied cats together by their tails.

Tomorrow, we'll read he once punched a hole
in the wall over a video game his mom took away—
he walked in circles, went days without bathing.

Soon, we can sort the comments from strangers
on the internet into a single category:
Just look at those dead eyes, everyone says
as the family's Christmas photo from Facebook goes viral.

No one asks, *Did the cats untie their own tails?*

Who buried the broken frogs, then washed their hands?

When You Say People Mistake Motion for Progress

You mean my mother
who drove north from Tampa
on U.S. 41 in a faded red
Ford from 1974 and didn't stop
until she'd reached the tip
of the Keweenaw Peninsula.
You mean the mother who emailed
my work address, which she found
online, to say she'd been sober
for a year and learned to respect
other people's boundaries.
You mean the mother who sent
a photo of my niece I never ask about
because I never knew she existed
because I've never met my brother
and *why don't I care about my family.*

Somewhere there is a salmon
who is tired of swimming upstream,
who chooses to stay at sea, where
she flourishes, rather than return
to the river of her birth, where
the work of digging redds awaits,
where there will be fighting
and graveled flesh, where
she will die once she's laid her eggs.

Decimation

When God gets angry, he goes all out.

There's no come-to-Jesus meeting
in Genesis; just rain, lots of rain, until
everyone drowns in their sin.
No mystery as to *why*. God makes it clear:
The earth is corrupt and full of violence.
Noah is spared, plus two of each creature
and a bunch of clean animals for sacrifice.
The rainbow after the flood doesn't promise
safety—only that *next* time, the world won't end
with water. There are so many ways to die.

The Book of Numbers is a warning—
poisonous snakes feast on dissidents;
fire falls from the sky; the earth opens
its mouth to swallow rebels; plague after
plague consumes Israel until she complies.
In 471 BC, the Roman Republic uses
decimation for punishment. Consider it
a perverse tithe, offering the unclean
as sacrifice to save the rest—it makes sense.
We can't afford annihilation.

They say decimation isn't used anymore
despite rumors during the Great War,
but Life has a way of keeping us in line.
I think of family, the cohort marriage made
and try to decide which of us drew
the short straw. Think of the soldier
who survives to see a tenth of his unit
executed for the crime he committed.
Is it luck we are spared? We keep living,
ever as dead as the ones picked to die.

Before the Apocalypse, Sentries Abandon Post

Supposedly, we all have an editor in our head—clicking backspace, altering the script. Somebody always on the lookout. So I wonder where the guardian angel was when God created the locust and the termite, the mosquito. Nobody said a word. They just let him do his thing, watched as he proclaimed it was good, even though he knew what would happen to Pharaoh and to my grandmother's house; how many people would die from malaria.

And I wonder where the angel was a decade ago when I said *I do*. Nobody tried to stop me from walking down the aisle, not even when the preacher gave the crowd a final chance. Where is the censor now when Mother tells me to put on lipstick—*You need some color in your face, to draw the eye; that hairstyle does you no favors.*

If God ever looks at Earth from his celestial throne, he doesn't see green and blue melded hues—beautiful lies the satellites send us from space. The whole planet is a giant plumber, bent over hard at work, trying to fix pipes that broke in the Flood. And we're just tiny drops of sweat, proof of labor, rolling insignificantly from one part of the world to another, hoping something will save us from being wiped away.

Bones

In my hand is a chicken bone my mama calls a wishbone.
She says if two people each take a different side
and pull until the bones break—
the person with the bigger splinter makes a wish.

Right now, the horseshoe-shaped stem is whole as my hand
cups its sides of equal length—two bones that by chance
or design have merged into one like the apex
of Florida and Nebraska Avenues, now Highway 41.

I wonder if wishes really come from the dried bones.
I wonder who I can pick a bone with.

If All My Dreams Came True

IV.

Some Things Are Decided Before You Are Born

Doctors cannot tell you
when you're born
how many pitches your arm
contains. But they know rounds
are already loaded, ready
for firing, long before you tie
your shoes or write your name
and discover you're a righty.

It's like eggs in an ovary: Even if
they are never used, the body
cannot hold onto them forever.
A finite number determined by DNA,
it's impossible to know how many
chances you have, and when
you will run out.

No one can tell you how
the first hundred pitches will be
spent on backyard games, throwing
penny-weighted wine corks wrapped
in tape twenty feet to Bobby Talbot,
his broken broom ready to send
your fastball to the fence.

Or how the next thousand will be
a mix of change-ups and curveballs—
playing little league on Davis Island,
showing off for debutantes
on the boulevard. Throwing strikes
will be easier than getting to first base
with Leela Howard.

Strasburg and Smoltz are proof
players come back after injury.
The thing that kills a man
is watching his star
slowly drop from the sky.
There's no Cy Young Award
for a man who sells real estate,
no matter how good you are.

These days, people might
think you walk around during
your grandson's game because
you're too old to sit for seven
innings straight, something about
metal bleachers being no good
for the back. Maybe it's
your prostate.

But it's just your legs
missing the windup—the high kick
from standstill into motion,
the unfurling of power.
It's the long march toward rebirth:
King of the Hill once more,
daring batters to blink, to swing.

Parenting by Peripatetic Fragments

Because I think too much
my tween son gives me word limits
when he wants quick answers
to his questions about Life.

He's right: I forget our words
are just the vehicle, taking us
where we want to go. Too often,
I get stuck on the sentence, hold
tight to language, won't let loose.

Who refuses to deplane
after the captain turns off
the seat belt sign? Life is waiting
outside the airtight cabin, willing
us to push aside the clouds and
jump in the wind.

...

I can tell by the sliver of moon
God's been clipping his toenails.
My father taught me this.

During downpours,
Dad would say, *Uh-oh*
the devil's beatin' his wife.
Light showers: *God's sneezing.*

My dad was a regular Aristotle.
When I threatened to run away:
No matter where you go,
there you are. When I made excuses

after losing a tennis match: *If a frog had wings,*
he wouldn't bump his butt when he landed.

At middle age, I still hear my dad
when it rains or the moon's anything
less than full, when my son cuts his steak
in bites too big, when I want to run away.

Tell me—   who will teach me to be old?
Who will hold my hand to cross this street?
Who will show my son how to play defense,
how to sink a skyhook from outside the key?

Housebroken

Now starts the slow domestication,
the unloved urgency

of getting the job done. It doesn't matter
what my job is— or yours.

We do it.

And if we're ever in doubt,
our kids will tell us what's wrong
with the world and exactly how to fix it.

And we'll pretend we're listening

to them the way our parents did with us,
knowing smugly— and sadly,
that someday they, too,

will sit in a driver's seat and nod.

Blessed Are the Peacemakers

God did not send an angel to my husband, telling him I would conceive a son. God did not tell me to name him John. I named him John anyway, after an ancestor who signed the Declaration of Independence. Baby John was circumcised on the third day and home under bilirubin lights by the eighth. Queen Elizabeth II was on the throne—she did not order him to be killed. And so he would be permitted to live past two years old, if he was lucky enough to escape the current threat.

And when he was thirteen months old, there in stroller, I took Baby John with me to buy meat at the deli. We were second in line. The woman in front turned around, said she hoped John would stay little forever, never grow up to fight in one of Bush's wars. The aproned man behind the counter selling pulled pork stood to his full height and decreed: *John will be a peacemaker.*

At thirteen, John is still growing into his name, still learning what it means to be a child of God. Peace is easier for the meek. At thirteen, John has not yet inherited the earth—for there is too much Fortnite and hormones and rebelling against Miss Collins' rules in civics class. Middle school and puberty conspire against his calling. Still, grace abounds.

Blessed is this boy, for he shall inherit my calves, my curiosity, my habit of washing hands. Along with these gifts, he will also inherit his father's baller skills, eyebrows, constellatory moles. The boy shall inherit his family's love of board games and play Monopoly with the temptation to pass Go and collect more than $200. The boy will grow as the years allow, fed by sunlight and rainfall—fruit chews, pancakes, and sharp cheddar cheese. Someday, he will take stock of all that his parents and this world have left him, remember the prophecy and make his choice.

Making Confession

Only in the doctor's office
will I tell a complete stranger
what sex feels like. Slowly
shed my shyness like skin,
let her in—but hold my breath
tight in a cocoon of fear,
jaw and body clenched
against new pain.

Until she says *breathe* and
suddenly
it's the last day of school
before summer
before white sand
before Longboat Key
before the kite flies high
in the breeze.

I sink into the table, held
to earth by stirrups—
too tired to gallop away
from diagnosis, to untangle
kite tails knotted in trees,
to protect butterfly wings
from hands too eager
to touch.

Anatomies of Difference

You wake me again tonight
with a start—you, still asleep
me, a sideline spectator, watching
your semi-frozen legs race
beneath the sheets. You are running
the way you used to, before
bone death boxed your medals
on a closet shelf too high to reach.

In the dark, I see your shadow
ready at his mark. Quadriceps
coil—pause—and unload
their pressure onto the knee,
down a once-chiseled calf,
to the Achilles tendon and
foot strike, as the pistol
crack splits the sky.

You are spent—
sprawled, wrapped in ribbons
of sweat, the sheets a shroud.
I map damp tendrils in rain-
soaked woodsy trails, swathes
of scarred skin, these fallen
limbs, and tap your thighs
in soft applause as your
stride slows to rest.

Here lie anatomies
of difference—between
the man who was and
the man who is, the man you are
and the woman I might be.
I, too, live in dreams.

After the Diagnosis

Don't think of this as a dark night
of the soul but as a pool
in the backyard, where children
once played, where grandkids
learn to swim. Where you go
alone sometimes just to cool off,
relax. Calm winded-waves,
the pale blue surface lit
by relentless stars in a black sky.

Consider your body in the water—
the way the water holds your weight
and invites you under—like a return
to the amniotic sac, where lungs
don't require air, where the dark
feels like home, where every sound
is soft music, even the machines,
the whir of a doctor's voice.

Don't think of what might happen:
how cells multiply in the dark, how
the body rebels without warning.
Instead, insist your body move
beneath the deep—despite the ache,
the burn of lungs that swell with fear.

Consider the stars a swimmer sees
right before his lungs burst,
right before he breaks the surface
and swallows air instead of water,
gulping salvation. Think of
constellations, the way certain light
shimmers across a pin-pricked sky.

Chronic

Have you ever just hurt and hurt and hurt and
hurt until you were tired of hurting
so tired you would give anything to stop hurting
give anything to sleep through the night

give your money to anyone with steady hands
give your clothes to women who go to work
give your amethyst to Isabelle with the pretty name
pendants are for girls who have use for pretty
pretty is a memory too heavy to lift

give your pens to someone with words to write
whose thoughts aren't mosquitoes zapped by machines
give your kaleidoscope collection to anyone
who can look at the light without shrieking

give the heirloom clock in the hall to Dan
who likes watches and is hard of hearing—
it ticks too loud, a tell-tale heart you can hear
from anywhere in the house as you're waiting
for the sky to signal it's bedtime

waiting for the bed to get comfortable
waiting for something resembling sleep
that's all you need—you just know it
more than doctors who don't know anything

you only need to rest and you'd give anything—
everything—to fall asleep and wake up well

The Cone of Uncertainty

An irregular heartbeat has been detected,
says the smart watch—and I wonder
if this is the last sentence I'll ever read,
the last time I'll check the buzzing at my wrist.
What if I die here, on the back porch, where
I only sat to cool down, to dry off, after rain
turned a walk into a race. Behold this miracle
of movement! Faster than I've run in years,
darting through yards like deer, scared
of lightning, startled by tree limbs blown
by outer bands of summer, a violent storm
that will move on soon after the damage,
like seasons of marriage my mom warned
me about. I wait for the all-clear
so I can move again at a natural pace,
stopping to look at the red bird or flock
of clouds, imagining they're a heart, a smile
or cotton candy sweet in our mouth. Instead,
I melt into this chair, writing goodbyes
in my mind—another word with every blink,
every stuttered beat. Praying someone
finds me if I fall, as my whole body buzzes.

I Don't Want to Write Any More Poems

Because they don't do the important things,
the things Life depends on, like cooking dinner
or emptying the dishwasher. They won't fold
clothes or fill the car with gas or sit at a desk
eight hours a day, listening to the boss bark.
But then I read Moira Egan's *Hot Flash Sonnets*
as I wait for the doctor. Suddenly, a chuckle
is enough to face diagnosis. I wrap words
around my body like a cast, setting what's broken
so it can heal. At night, Rae Hoffman Jager stands
by me as I soothe my son, rocking away the croup
that seeps through bronchi like an invasive moon
through metal blinds. In this world, poems are
like women—unseen, the work often unpraised,
done in dark hours without witness, necessary
as sleep, as blood, as air.

In Each of Her Folds a Promise Waits

V.

Autodidacts

Colin touched me in high school
the way a boy sticks his hand
out the car window on road trips.
His hands were warm from
whatever it is boys do in their
pockets—move things around,
fiddle with keys. Even in a
backseat, there is revelation. I knew
then that my boobs were meant for
hands other than mine, for more
than nursing some future baby
the adult me might deliver.

In college, I learned how to turn
a dorm room into a tennis court.
How to lob a man after bringing him
to the net, how to serve out the set, how
to win love, love. Colin didn't complain
when I taught him to touch my tits
without using his hands. We practiced
being grownups, tried not to get hurt.

I warn my husband there can be blood
in breast milk. So says one of the books
stacked by our bed, each page marked
like the TripTiks I used to navigate
the nineties. *Breast-fed babies are more*
likely to succeed in life. I take notes.
Women who give birth before thirty

are less likely to develop breast cancer.
I buy a calendar, I plan. I forget
the body is a playground. Somewhere
Colin grows old with his wife and kids,
hands stuffed deep into empty pockets.

Loss by the Gallon

Painting the house is an act of forfeit.
Each brush stroke a soft surrender.
Swish then *wish,* then *swish,* then
some new color to cover up the divorce.
But underneath it all, it's still a wall—
always a wall. Don't believe the home
improvement ads. *Winsome Gray*
in the bedroom won't end the argument.
Balmoral Red doesn't fix libido.
Ponder can't save the marriage.
Each layer we add dries. Efforts fade,
then peel. Small flecks the color of attempt
fall to a tile floor already chipped, grout
spotted and smudged beyond cleaning.

Visitation

When Abraham came by after work
to pick up Isaac and said he was taking him
hunting on Mt. Moriah, Sarah cautioned them
to be careful—

look out for mountain lions, please
ticks are everywhere this time of year
make sure he keeps the knife
pointed away from his body

Abraham nodded like normal,
without a word about the visitation,
his divine mission. She would only laugh
at such crazy talk, call Child & Family Services.

...

I remember Sarah when you swing by
on Father's Day for visitation.
You say you're taking our son
fishing in the Gulf of Mexico, and I warn
about sunscreen and sharks,
barnacles that slice to the bone.

I press a bag of worms, wet and dirty
from the garden, into his small hand
and whisper—

If Daddy says he forgot
to bring bait, stick these on the hook
just like I showed you, careful
not to prick your skin, careful
not to leave tracks he can follow
when you wriggle away.

I Will Never Be the Woman

on Twitter with a new haircut
and scarlet lips, crowing
about her divorce decree after
she danced home from the court-
house to post pics of her live-in lover.
Or the poet who writes pretty lines
about her divorce with words
her daughter whispered in a house
somewhere in Kansas. Too young
for the kitchen, the girl spills
flour on the floor. Mom sweeps
it into a bowl, kneads the mess
into dough, adds mascara tears,
pounds with fists calloused
in marriage—until she can twist
and twist and cook the lump
into metaphor that will sell.

There's no planting my son's words
or watching sobs grow into trees. No
pretending his pain holds up the sky.
I'm the woman who dreams of being
a war widow, telling everyone
my husband died in battle, or that he
woke up one morning and confessed
he was gay. Born in the wrong body.
If only discontent left a bruise
I could lift my shirt to show.

I will never be the woman
who eats ice cream in bed after sex—
straight from the pint propped on
a doughy stomach, naked rolls of fat

keeping the Half Baked steady.
I wear a robe after every shower,
even when I'm the only one home.

Running into My Ex at Publix

With all the hard pains passed
we stand in silence—two years
and shopping carts between us—
pretending to search for expected
friends, hoping some familiar face
will save us.

Without much to say
that hasn't already been said,
we swap half-smiles, ask
about deli deals.

Soon, we'll make polite excuses
and go different directions
at rush hour.

One learns to check fruit
for ripeness, feeling hard skin
for soft spots. One learns
to buy just enough—and to eat it
before it all goes bad.

Boomerang

When we let go of anything,
it's always with the secret hope
that whatever we once held
will one day come back to us.
This is a truth we don't like
to admit, even to ourselves.
We want to think we're being
generous, or zen, or wise

when we move
from the marriage bed
to the guest room.
But deep down we dream
of a future return, some kind
of restoration; otherwise,
we'd never let go—
not of our small child's hand,
not of a lover who's eager
to be someplace else,

not of the happy dream
that life could be better.
We treat our son's school
drop and every kiss goodbye
like waiting rooms, a temporary
holding place for everything

we love, trusting we will
get it all back soon enough—
healthy, whole.

But when the thing
does not return, the truth

we wouldn't admit
is made clear: We let it go
and wanted it to stay
and it was always both,
at the same time.

When the email warns
my rewards are expiring,
I want to rush out
and buy something,
anything. I can't bear
another loss. Not again.
Not even 300 points.

My son's hands are bigger
than mine now—he holds his phone,
a basketball, pencils with no erasers
because he's peeled them off.
He doesn't know yet that his hands
will never be big enough
or strong enough.

I don't have an answer
when he asks why I let go
of Daddy's hand. I think maybe
I made a mistake.
Because this life's not much
different from the life
I kissed goodbye years ago,
exhausted, thinking
it would someday return
to me—healthy, whole.

Daughter of the Revolution

My grandmother was born a mermaid.
What's a West Virginia coal miner to do
with a daughter who's a mermaid?

The Talbotts moved to Florida
and dropped a T to make a name
for themselves. Dot was the first
woman on athletic scholarship
at the University of Tampa, editor
for the school paper. She filled
the minarets with mischief.

She swam with Tarzan. Shot pistols
at Silver Springs. Made friends
with a herpetologist; took care
not to fall in love. Only swooned
at the sound of an ace, or swish.

After the diagnosis, doctors took
too much of her brain, leaving her
muscles paralyzed. Her young
husband left too.

Dot taught herself independence.
How to write. How to walk.
How to shine with only half
a smile. She taught her son

to be a man. Taught her granddaughter
to swim, to breathe between strokes,
to turn at the wall—

taught her that a woman
who wasn't born a mermaid can float
on rough water, how floating
can save a life.

A Single Gust Is All It Takes

If you tried to measure the distance
from department store clerk to customer
during Christmas that year, you'd first
need to account for the register
and countertop and the politeness
of 1946. The space between
customers is undeniably scarce—
breathless and thin like post-War
patrons who elbow for room to see
and be seen. You can measure the line
between husband and wife by the blue thread
her grandmother used to sew a bow
on the wedding garter, a thing now yellowed
like dreams. The line between bricks outside
on Tampa Street is a crack no one dare step on.
Vendors sell popcorn to a shiny mob
of inline six engines parked on Zack.
Boys play stickball in the street, stepping
on manhole covers, tagging a delivery truck
as they run for home. The line between
the start of a dream and the end
is too thin to measure. A single gust
is all it takes to break the thread
that stitches us together.

Things We've Handed Down

Where it all ends I can't fathom, my friends
If I knew, I might toss out my anchor
—Jimmy Buffet, "Son of a Son of a Sailor"

My grandfather was an obstetrician;
his father a lawyer on Franklin Street;
his father brought artesian wells to Alabama.
Just like the Bible, I know little
of the women—
mothers and grandmothers left out
of the genealogy. Women are changed
by marriage; forgotten footnotes
hard to track in the census. Except
when the last will and testament lists
us with the horses, furniture, pots and pans.

Yet when my brother turned fifty, I knew
I still wanted to be like him—
the way I did when we were kids.
Even when he put his cologne on
my favorite stuffed animal—a horse
named Lightning, who forever smelled
like a teenage boy masking the stench
of puberty. Even when he was punished
for sneaking out of the house and taking
our dad's Pontiac to a party. I never

went to parties. Never climbed
out the window into the dog's side yard
even when I wanted to. I wanted to
travel to China, land a high-paying job, sail
the Gulf of Mexico. I want to be brave
like my big brother, who was always good

at math and had the best handwriting;
who always knew what he wanted
and how to get it—and still does
for the most part. At fifty, he knows
there are some things we never get,
no matter how much we want them.

The Last Goodbye's the Hardest

If there were a horse we could ride
into the sunset, like John Wayne
before closing credits, like George Strait
sings from the stage—he would be
named Docs Poco Dynamite
and he'd never win a single race.
Doc would be a working horse, at ease
under the saddle, happy to see the barn,
the farm, the cowboy he loves best.

If there were a dog who got along
with horses, who loved the woods
and the Wild West, who tracked ducks
like he was gifted by the gods,
we'd call him Tex and he would jump
in the truck before sun-up, ready
for the ride, any ride.

If there were a brother who scattered
the sting of childhood around the
cul-de-sac and down the lonely street,
who made room for a girl to play
football and put her on the shirts team,
we would call him Bubs and we
would draw plays on our stomach
in the backyard huddle and we'd run
and pass and tackle like the 1984
Raiders and never forget as long
as we lived.

Wait for Me

Someday, when I have stopped feeling sad,
I will tell you a story. About the helicopter
spiraling into a skyscraper. About chin hairs
plucked in car lines. About the mom who left.
Someday, when you are old, I will tell you
what it's like to be old. About the neck that stops
turning to check for traffic. About the body
that wants to be eyed by strangers. The mouth—
how it puckers for no reason. Someday,
when you are ready to listen, you will hear
how I wore ears from the gun range and shut
myself in the study to work, how Xbox trigger
fingers still drummed into poems, why the rusted
feeder out back hasn't been filled in years. Someday,
when I have stopped worrying about the world,
I will smile. You will know I am happy.

Fagaceae Quercus Virginiana

When someone says *broken*
family they mean broken
like a promise, like a bone,
like a dish. It will hurt
to think of us this way.
Instead, think of travelers
leaving one land for another
learning to speak a broken
language, tongue halting
and full of stories.
Remember the acorns
you collected by the fistfuls
in toddler paws, calling them
a-torns until your tongue
learned articulation.
Remember the big oak
on Old Pasco Road, how
its branches were split
like a wishbone
to make room for utility wires.
I won't tell you the tree
wasn't hurt by the blade or isn't
pained each time it's trimmed
into some new shape;
that it doesn't save its wince
until dark, scream in a pitch
far beyond our human ears.
But see how the tree still grows—
arms full of birds and squirrels,
clothed heavy in leaves and seed.

Skipping Stones

Because I'm tired of being angry
at the world, I take my son to the river
where we pick up rocks at the water's edge—
both of us wrapped tight in Christmas
gifts, chest and arms warm
in this year's already bitter weather.
We step in shallows
where cold water's still clear, searching
through sediment for stones.

Here I teach him to choose
smooth, triangular stones—for stability,
how to weigh the rock by lifting it
up and down, up and down
in hands he will grow into:
Too heavy and the rock will sink;
too light and you'll lose it in the wind.

Like David, the teenager minding sheep
for his father, picked rocks to protect his flock
from the lion or the bear—my boy listens,
learns what to keep and what to leave
buried in the mud. He already knows
that quickness, not strength, is key.

By the time he's old enough to drive,
he'll be an expert at skipping stones—
bending his arm just right,
balancing the flat rock's perfect heft
between thumb and middle finger,
his index hooked along the edge, ready
to fling a pebble with all his might
into the face of giants.

In Praise of Science & Silverados

I first read "Jump Cabling" in college
and knew I wanted a man like that:
a problem-solver, someone who would
be the red to my black, who would
know the importance of grounding
and how to make sparks fly. I loved
Pastan's poem long before I lived it,
before I knew a woman could die
and be brought back to life.

Now that I'm almost fifty, I remember
replicative senescence—something
my biology professor said years ago.
How long until my cells stop dividing?
How long before the body breaks down?

If you, the man in the silver Chevy truck,
are stranded, and I, the middle-aged woman
you met after the divorce, am stranded too—
praise be the telomere that ties us together.
Praise be the partner who grows old with me
while the tail that tethers us grows shorter
like days in winter. Praise be electricity
that warms the body, that lights the dark
from now until this body is done
and darkness is all there is.

Reduplication

We make our intentions
clear when we repeat
the words: I like you,
but I don't *like you-like you.*
Or we say again for emphasis,
to give the body something
to punctuate: You really,
really need to stop. Please,
please don't go.

Couples easily recognize love
as work but admit it's not
work-work. With children,
we double the word to halve
the pain—softly scold a *no-no,*
kiss away the *boo-boo.*

It's the *hubba-hubba*
of spring that turns us
into parents. Then we take
our turn as *Mimi* or *Papa,*
a parent-parent. We sit
on the porch, listen to trees
murmur. The little ones
throw leaves like confetti
at a going away party and
suddenly we're walking
our daughter down the aisle,
running beside her new bike,
standing over the cradle—
whispering *there, there.*

We all learn to wave
bye-bye before we know
what the word means,
or how to say it.

Acknowledgments

Special thanks to the editors and publications where many of these poems first appeared, sometimes under a different title or in a different form: *Aethlon: The Journal of Sport Literature, After the Pause, Amaryllis, Amethyst Review, Atrium Poetry, Barren Magazine, Bonnie's Crew, Chasing Light Anthology, Clear Poetry, Constellate Literary Journal, Dirty Paws Poetry, Easy Street, Eunoia Review, First Things, Four Ties Lit Review, Gyroscope Review, Halfway Down the Stairs, Hoctok Magazine, Helen, Ink, Sweat & Tears, Kissing Dynamite, Likely Red, Middle House Review, Mother's Always Write, Muddy River Poetry Review, Nine Muses, Okay Donkey, Picaroon Poetry, Plum Tree Tavern, Psaltery & Lyre, Rat's Ass Review, Rust + Moth, Sandhill Review, Solstice Sounds, Stoneboat Literary Journal, Sweet, SWWIM Every Day, The Coil, The Ekphrastic Review, The Furious Gazelle, The Lascaux Review, The Opiate, The UCity Review, Unbroken Journal, War, Literature & the Arts,* and *Whale Road Review.*

The title "The Happy Hour of Assault" is taken from a translated line in Pablo Neruda's poem "The Song of Despair." Hat tip to Robert Frost, who once said, "Poetry is a way of taking life by the throat." The title "Love Is Not Love" is borrowed from Shakespeare's Sonnet 116. The line *Dulce et decorum est pro patria mori*, originally from Horace's Odes (III.2.13), is used in Wilfred Owen's poem *Dulce et Decorum Est* and is roughly translated as, "It is sweet and right to die for one's country." The title "History Is Now and England" is a line from T.S. Eliot's poem "Little Gidding" in *Four Quartets.*

I am forever indebted to several people who were teachers to me in title and by example: Lorraine Craven, Brena Walker, Adrienne Bond, Mary Wilder, Will D. Campbell, Joe Hendricks, Tom Trimble, Dana Gioia, Tony Cooke, and Sara M. Deats.

Particular thanks are due to these journal editors who believed in my early work and answered my questions about the literary world with patient kindness: Roderick Bates, Genna Rivieccio, Ben Banyard, Kate Garrett, and Reuben Woolley. I also owe thanks to the College English Association (especially Lynne Simpson), Popular Culture Association (especially Katie Manning), and South Atlantic Modern Language Association, whose conferences allowed me to present several of these poems—and to Saint Leo University for their professional development funds, which enabled me to attend these conferences and share my work.

I greatly appreciate the following folks, each a writer I admire, for generously reading these poems and giving me their thoughts: Stephen Parrish, Keith O'Shaughnessy, Jack Bedell, Deirdre Fagan, and Steve Kistulentz.

This book would not exist without the kindness and professionalism of Marc Jolley and his indomitable team at Mercer University Press. Go Bears.

I'm eternally grateful for the Creator, my Savior, the One who makes all things new.

Lastly, my heart is filled with gratitude for my family and loved ones (*especially* my mom, fiancé, and beloved son) who are undoubtedly my biggest fans and strongest supporters. I couldn't do this without them—and wouldn't want to.

About the Author

Marissa Glover earned her bachelor of arts degree at Mercer University in 1996, where she double-majored in English and philosophy and played on the tennis team. Marissa received her master's in English literature and a graduate certificate in creative writing from the University of South Florida and now teaches writing, humanities, and public speaking courses at Saint Leo University. Before entering academia, Marissa worked as a writer and editor for various companies for more than fifteen years.

Marissa is currently coeditor of *Orange Blossom Review* and a senior editor at *The Lascaux Review*. Her own writing has been widely published in various journals and anthologies, but her best work will always be on her parents' refrigerator. This is Marissa's first book of poetry.